Dream Jamaica: A Travel Guide.

Daniel Hunter

All rights reserved. No part of this publication may be reproduced, distributed, or transmitted in any form or by any means, including photocopying, recording, or other electronic or mechanical methods, without the prior written permission of the publisher, except in the case of brief quotations embodied in critical reviews and certain other noncommercial uses permitted by copyright law.

Copyright © (Daniel Hunter) (2024).

TABLE OF CONTENTS

Chapter I. Introduction — 5
    A. Welcome to Jamaica — 5
    B. Travel Tips and Essentials — 6

Chapter II. Solo Travelers — 9
    A. Safety Tips — 9
    B. Solo-Friendly Accommodations — 11
    C. Unique Experiences for Solo Travelers — 14

Chapter III. Family Travel — 17
    A. Kid-Friendly Activities — 17
    B. Family-Friendly Resorts — 19
    C. Practical Tips for Traveling with Kids — 21

Chapter IV. Couples Retreat — 25
    A. Romantic Beaches and Settings — 25
    B. Couple-Friendly Adventures — 27
    C. Intimate Dining and Nightlife — 29

Chapter V. Hidden Gems — 33
    A. Off-the-Beaten-Path Attractions — 33
    B. Local Favorites and Cultural Gems — 35
    C. Serene Nature Escapes — 37

Chapter VI. Must-Visit Locations — 41
    A. Iconic Landmarks — 41
    B. Historical Sites — 43
    C. Scenic Spots — 45

Chapter VII. Itineraries — 49
    A. One-Week Adventure — 49
    B. Weekend Getaway Plans — 50
    C. Customizable Itinerary Options — 53

Chapter VIII. Culinary Delights   **57**
    A. Jamaican Cuisine Overview   57
    B. Best Local Eateries   59
    C. Street Food Exploration   61

Chapter IX. Transportation and Getting Around 65
    A. Transportation Options   65
    B. Tips for Navigating Jamaica   67

Chapter X. Cultural Insights   **71**
    A. Jamaican Traditions   71
    B. Festivals and Events   73
    C. Interacting with Locals   76

Chapter XI. Practical Information   **79**
    A. Currency and Money Matters   79
    B. Health and Safety   81
    C. Communication Essentials   83
    D. Emergency Contacts   86

Chapter XII. Conclusion   **88**
    A. Share your experience   88

Celestial Rhythms: The Legend of Jamaica's Harmony Stones   **91**

Chapter I. Introduction

A. *Welcome to Jamaica*

Welcome to the vibrant island of Jamaica, a tropical paradise where lush landscapes meet the rhythmic beats of reggae, and the warm hospitality of the locals invites you to experience the true essence of the Caribbean. In this comprehensive travel guide, we invite you to embark on an unforgettable journey through the heart and soul of Jamaica. Whether you're a solo adventurer, a family seeking fun-filled activities, or a couple in search of romance, this guide is crafted to cater to every traveler's desires. Join us as we explore hidden gems, unveil must-visit locations, and provide curated itineraries that promise an authentic Jamaican experience. From the sun-kissed beaches to the vibrant cultural scene, let this guide be your companion as you discover the enchanting beauty and rich heritage that make Jamaica a captivating destination for all. Get ready to immerse yourself in the laid-back charm, adventure, and warmth that define the spirit of Jamaica.

B. Travel Tips and Essentials

When embarking on your Jamaican adventure, it's essential to be well-prepared to fully savor the island's vibrant culture and breathtaking landscapes. Here are some travel tips and must-have essentials to ensure a smooth and enjoyable experience:

1. Pack Light and Comfortable:
   Jamaica's tropical climate calls for light, breathable clothing. Don't forget swimwear, sunblock, and a hat for protection against the Caribbean sun.

2. Stay Hydrated:
   The warmth can be intense, so keep yourself hydrated by drinking plenty of water throughout the day. Consider carrying a reusable water bottle to reduce environmental impact.

3. Local Currency and Cash:
   While credit cards are widely accepted, having some Jamaican dollars on hand for local markets and small vendors is advisable. ATMs are available in major towns and tourist areas.

4. Safety First:
   Jamaica is generally safe, but it's wise to stay vigilant. Keep valuables secure, use reputable transportation, and be cautious in unfamiliar areas, especially at night.

5. Immerse in Local Culture:
   Respect Jamaican customs and traditions. Learn a few basic phrases in Patois (local Jamaican dialect) to connect with locals and enhance your cultural experience.

6. Transportation Choices:
   Explore the island's beauty with a mix of transportation options. Taxis, rental cars, and organized tours offer diverse ways to discover hidden gems and popular attractions.

7. Weather Awareness:
   Jamaica experiences a tropical climate, with a rainy season from May to October. Check the weather forecast and plan activities accordingly, but don't let occasional rain dampen your spirits—Jamaica is beautiful in any weather.

8. Health Precautions:
   Pack necessary medications and consider travel insurance that covers medical emergencies.

Mosquito repellent can be handy, especially in more rural areas.

9. Island Time:
Embrace the relaxed pace of life in Jamaica. Locals operate on "island time," so be patient and enjoy the laid-back atmosphere.

10. Connect with Locals:
Engage with the friendly locals; they are a valuable source of information on hidden gems and authentic experiences. Building connections can enrich your journey.

Remember, preparation is key, but flexibility and openness to the unexpected will make your Jamaican adventure truly unforgettable. Embrace the rhythm of the island and let the vibrant spirit of Jamaica captivate you.

Chapter II. Solo Travelers

A. *Safety Tips*

Safety Tips for Solo Travelers in Jamaica:

1. Choose Accommodations Wisely:
   Opt for reputable accommodations with positive reviews, ensuring a safe and secure environment for your stay. Look for well-reviewed guesthouses, boutique hotels, or resorts known for their commitment to guest safety.

2. Stay Informed About Neighborhoods:
   Research and be aware of the safety reputation of different neighborhoods. Avoid poorly lit or deserted areas, especially at night. Stick to well-populated and tourist-friendly areas for added security.

3. Local Transportation Awareness:
   Use official and recognized transportation services. If using public transportation, stay vigilant and be cautious of personal belongings. Consider using reputable ride-sharing apps for convenience and safety.

4. Keep Valuables Secure:

Minimize the jewelry and valuables you carry. Use a money belt or hidden pouch for important documents, such as your passport and extra cash. Be discreet with your belongings to avoid attracting unwanted attention.

5. Stay Connected:
Keep your loved ones informed about your whereabouts. Share your itinerary with someone trustworthy and regularly check in with them. Having a local SIM card or an international roaming plan ensures you can communicate easily.

6. Be Aware of Local Customs:
Familiarize yourself with Jamaican cultural norms and customs. Respecting local traditions can contribute to a positive experience and minimize misunderstandings.

7. Trust Your Instincts:
If a situation feels uncomfortable or unsafe, trust your instincts and remove yourself from it. Avoid confrontation and seek assistance from authorities or reputable establishments if needed.

8. Blend In with Local Attire:
Dress modestly and in a way that aligns with local customs. This not only shows respect for the culture

but also helps you avoid standing out as a tourist, reducing the risk of becoming a target for scams or theft.

9. Nighttime Caution:
   Exercise caution when venturing out after dark. Stick to well-lit areas and consider using reputable transportation services rather than walking alone at night.

10. Emergency Contacts and Services:
    Save local emergency numbers and contact information for your country's embassy or consulate. Familiarize yourself with nearby medical facilities and know the location of police stations.

Remember, while Jamaica is a beautiful destination, staying informed and exercising caution enhances your solo travel experience. Always prioritize your safety and well-being.

B. Solo-Friendly Accommodations

Traveling solo in Jamaica provides a unique opportunity for self-discovery, and choosing the right accommodation can enhance this experience. Here are some solo-friendly options that cater to the needs and preferences of solo travelers:

1. Boutique Hotels and Guesthouses:
   - Opt for intimate boutique hotels or guesthouses that offer a personalized and cozy atmosphere.
   - These accommodations often provide a chance to connect with fellow travelers in communal spaces.

2. Hostels with Social Spaces:
   - Choose hostels that emphasize socializing with common areas, group activities, and organized tours.
   - Shared dormitories create a communal vibe, making it easy to meet like-minded travelers.

3. All-Inclusive Resorts with Solo Packages:
   - Some all-inclusive resorts offer special packages for solo travelers, providing a hassle-free experience.
   - Look for resorts that organize group activities and excursions for guests traveling alone.

4. Vacation Rentals and Homestays:
   - Opt for vacation rentals or homestays to experience local life and have a more private space.
   - Platforms like Airbnb often have options where hosts are open to interacting with solo guests.

5. Wellness Retreats and Eco-Lodges:

- Consider wellness retreats or eco-lodges that focus on holistic well-being and connecting with nature.
- These accommodations often have communal spaces for yoga, meditation, and group activities.

6. Safety-Conscious Hotels:
- Prioritize hotels in safe neighborhoods, and inquire about security measures in place.
- Many accommodations have 24/7 front desk services to ensure a secure environment for solo travelers.

7. Solo Traveler Hostels:
- Seek out hostels specifically designed for solo travelers, providing an environment geared towards individual exploration.
- These hostels often have social events and activities to facilitate connections among solo guests.

When choosing accommodations as a solo traveler in Jamaica, consider your preferences for social interaction, safety, and the type of experience you seek. Whether you prefer a tranquil retreat or a lively atmosphere, Jamaica offers a range of solo-friendly options to make your stay memorable.

C. Unique Experiences for Solo Travelers

For solo travelers seeking memorable experiences in Jamaica, the island offers a plethora of unique adventures that cater to the independent explorer.

1. Blue Mountain Hike and Coffee Tour:
   Embark on a solo journey to the majestic Blue Mountains, where you can trek through lush trails and visit coffee plantations. Indulge in the world-renowned Jamaican Blue Mountain coffee while enjoying breathtaking panoramic views.

2. River Rafting on the Martha Brae:
   Solo travelers can embrace tranquility by navigating the Martha Brae River on a bamboo raft. The serene journey through the lush Jamaican countryside offers a peaceful escape and a chance to connect with nature.

3. Reggae Music Immersion:
   Immerse yourself in Jamaica's rich musical culture by exploring Kingston's vibrant reggae scene. Visit iconic music studios, attend live performances, and feel the rhythmic heartbeat of reggae in its birthplace.

4. Local Culinary Safari:

Dive into the heart of Jamaican cuisine by exploring local markets, street food stalls, and authentic eateries. Solo travelers can engage with friendly locals, sample traditional dishes like jerk chicken and ackee and saltfish, and savor the island's flavors.

5. Blue Hole Exploration in Ocho Rios:
Solo adventurers can discover the hidden gem of the Blue Hole, a natural limestone sinkhole surrounded by tropical rainforest. Take a refreshing dip in its azure waters, explore caves, and cliff dive for an adrenaline rush.

6. Bob Marley Museum Excursion:
Pay homage to the legendary reggae icon by visiting the Bob Marley Museum in Kingston. Solo travelers can delve into Marley's life and legacy, surrounded by his music, personal artifacts, and the vibrant spirit of reggae.

7. Luminous Lagoon Night Tour:
Experience the magic of Glistening Waters, where a natural phenomenon creates a bioluminescent glow in the water. A night tour offers solo travelers the chance to witness this enchanting spectacle, creating a truly unique and mesmerizing memory.

Solo travelers in Jamaica can seamlessly blend adventure, culture, and relaxation, making their journey an unforgettable exploration of the island's diverse offerings.

Chapter III. Family Travel

A. Kid-Friendly Activities

Jamaica offers a plethora of kid-friendly activities, ensuring that families can create lasting memories together. From exciting adventures to educational experiences, here are some highlights:

1. Beach Fun:
   Introduce your kids to the pristine beaches of Jamaica. Seven Mile Beach in Negril and Doctor's Cave Beach in Montego Bay are ideal for building sandcastles, playing beach games, and enjoying crystal-clear waters.

2. Dolphin Cove:
   Head to Dolphin Cove for an unforgettable marine experience. Kids can swim with dolphins, interact with stingrays, and explore the park's lush surroundings.

3. Green Grotto Caves:
   Delve into the fascinating Green Grotto Caves in St. Ann, where your family can embark on an underground adventure. Marvel at the unique rock formations and learn about the caves' historical significance.

4. Mystic Mountain:

For an exhilarating day out, visit Mystic Mountain in Ocho Rios. Kids can soar through the treetops on the Sky Explorer chairlift, take a thrilling bobsled ride, and explore the educational butterfly and hummingbird gardens.

5. YS Falls:

Experience the beauty of YS Falls, a natural wonder surrounded by lush vegetation. Families can cool off in the cascading waterfalls, take a dip in the natural pools, and enjoy a picnic in the scenic surroundings.

6. Bob Marley Museum:

Introduce your kids to the legendary reggae icon at the Bob Marley Museum in Kingston. The interactive exhibits and vibrant atmosphere make it an engaging and educational experience for the entire family.

7. Pirate's Paradise Water Park:

Located in Ocho Rios, Pirate's Paradise Water Park promises a day of water-filled excitement. With thrilling slides, lazy rivers, and a dedicated children's area, it's a perfect spot for some family-friendly splashing fun.

8. Jamaican Bobsled Experience:
Channel the Cool Runnings spirit with a visit to the Rainforest Adventures Mystic Mountain. Kids can enjoy the Jamaican bobsled ride, inspired by the famous movie, offering a unique and entertaining adventure.

Jamaica's diverse attractions ensure that families with children of all ages can find activities that cater to both fun and education, making it an ideal destination for an unforgettable family vacation.

B. Family-Friendly Resorts

Jamaica offers an array of family-friendly resorts, ensuring an unforgettable Caribbean experience for every member of your family. Here's a glimpse into the enchanting world of family-oriented accommodations:

1. Beaches Negril Resort & Spa:
   - Located on the renowned Seven Mile Beach, this all-inclusive resort caters specifically to families.
   - Supervised kids' camps, engaging water parks, and themed character activities make it ideal for children of all ages.
   - Parents can indulge in spa treatments or explore a variety of dining options while the little ones enjoy the Kids Camp.

2. Franklyn D. Resort & Spa:
   - Known for its exceptional service, this Falmouth-based resort provides each family with a personal vacation nanny, offering parents some well-deserved relaxation.
   - Water sports, on-site activities, and spacious family suites contribute to a stress-free vacation for everyone.

3. Jewel Runaway Bay Beach & Golf Resort:
   - Nestled on the northern coast, this resort boasts a water park, a golf course, and a plethora of activities suitable for all ages.
   - With multiple dining options and evening entertainment, families can create lasting memories together.

4. Moon Palace Jamaica:
   - Situated in Ocho Rios, this expansive resort features a FlowRider® Double Wave Simulator, a family-friendly pool with water slides, and a kids' club.
   - From world-class dining to daily entertainment, the resort ensures a seamless blend of relaxation and excitement for the entire family.

5. Half Moon, Montego Bay:

- A timeless gem, Half Moon offers a perfect blend of luxury and family-oriented amenities.

- The Anancy Children's Village, equestrian center, and water sports cater to various interests, promising an enriching experience for every family member.

These family-friendly resorts in Jamaica not only provide a tropical haven but also create an environment where families can bond, explore, and create cherished memories together.

C. *Practical Tips for Traveling with Kids*

Traveling to Jamaica with your children promises a vibrant and enriching experience. To ensure a smooth and enjoyable family vacation, consider these practical tips:

1. Family-Friendly Accommodations:
   Choose accommodations that cater to families, offering amenities like kid-friendly pools, play areas, and babysitting services. Many resorts in Jamaica provide special programs and activities for children, ensuring both parents and kids have a memorable stay.

2. Health Precautions:

Prioritize your child's health by carrying necessary medications and familiarizing yourself with local healthcare facilities. It's advisable to bring insect repellent for protection against mosquitoes, especially in tropical areas.

3. Sun Protection:
The Caribbean sun can be intense. Pack sunscreen with a high SPF, hats, and sunglasses to shield your children from the sun's rays. Ensure they stay hydrated by encouraging frequent water breaks.

4. Adventure Planning:
Tailor your itinerary to include family-friendly attractions and activities. From interactive wildlife experiences to water parks, Jamaica offers a range of options suitable for different age groups. Consider the interests and energy levels of your kids when planning excursions.

5. Cultural Engagement:
Introduce your children to the rich Jamaican culture through interactive experiences. Attend local events, explore markets, and engage with friendly locals. This not only provides educational opportunities but also creates lasting memories for your family.

6. Local Cuisine Exploration:

While Jamaican cuisine is known for its bold flavors, there are options for even the pickiest eaters. Encourage your kids to try local fruits and dishes, but also have familiar snacks on hand. Many restaurants offer kid-friendly menus.

7. Safety Awareness:

Teach your children basic safety guidelines for exploring new environments. Establish a meeting point in case you get separated and ensure they know how to contact local authorities or resort staff in case of emergencies.

8. Packing Essentials:

Besides the usual travel essentials, pack items specifically for your kids, such as favorite toys, books, and comfort items. Having familiar items can ease the transition to a new environment.

9. Flexible Schedule:

Allow for flexibility in your daily schedule. Kids may need more downtime or have unexpected bursts of energy. Be open to adjusting plans to accommodate their needs, ensuring a more relaxed and enjoyable vacation for the entire family.

By incorporating these practical tips into your family travel plan, you'll be well-prepared to create wonderful memories in Jamaica with your children.

Chapter IV. Couples Retreat

A. Romantic Beaches and Settings

Nestled along the picturesque coastline of Jamaica, the island offers an array of romantic beaches and settings that set the stage for unforgettable moments with your significant other. Here's a glimpse into the enchanting world of Jamaican romance by the sea.

1. Seven Mile Beach, Negril:
   Sink your toes into the soft, golden sands of Seven Mile Beach in Negril, renowned for its breathtaking sunsets. This expansive stretch of shoreline provides a dreamy setting for a leisurely stroll with your loved one, hand in hand.

2. Frenchman's Cove, Port Antonio:
   Tucked away in Port Antonio, Frenchman's Cove is a secluded paradise surrounded by lush greenery. The river meets the sea here, creating a unique fusion of fresh and saltwater. Enjoy a private picnic or simply bask in the serenity of this hidden gem.

3. Blue Lagoon, Portland:
   Famous for its azure waters and mystical allure, the Blue Lagoon in Portland is a romantic haven. Take a boat ride across the captivating lagoon or

enjoy a quiet moment on its shores, surrounded by the emerald beauty of the surrounding hills.

4. Treasure Beach, St. Elizabeth:
   For couples seeking a laid-back atmosphere and authentic Jamaican charm, Treasure Beach in St. Elizabeth is a perfect choice. Unspoiled and tranquil, this beach offers a serene escape, allowing you to savor intimate moments away from the bustling crowds.

5. Lover's Leap, St. Elizabeth:
   Perched atop towering cliffs with panoramic views of the Caribbean Sea, Lover's Leap is a dramatic setting for romance. Legend has it that two runaway slaves leaped to their demise, choosing love over captivity. Today, the site offers a stunning backdrop for couples to create their own love story.

Whether it's the rhythmic sound of waves, the soft glow of sunset, or the seclusion of hidden coves, Jamaica's romantic beaches beckon lovers to create memories that will last a lifetime. Each location holds a unique charm, inviting couples to immerse themselves in the magic of the island's romantic allure.

B. Couple-Friendly Adventures

For couples seeking unforgettable experiences in Jamaica, the island offers a plethora of romantic adventures. From enchanting landscapes to thrilling activities, here are some couple-friendly adventures that promise to create lasting memories:

1. Sunset Catamaran Cruises:
   Set sail on the crystal-clear Caribbean waters aboard a romantic catamaran cruise. Witness the breathtaking Jamaican sunset as you and your partner enjoy the gentle breeze, sip on tropical cocktails, and embrace the beauty of the coast.

2. Dunn's River Falls Excursion:
   Embark on a hand-in-hand journey up the iconic Dunn's River Falls. This natural wonder provides a unique and exhilarating experience as you navigate the terraced limestone steps together, surrounded by lush greenery and cascading water.

3. Horseback Riding on the Beach:
   Explore Jamaica's scenic coastline on horseback, creating a dreamy and intimate atmosphere. Ride along the sandy shores, through tropical forests, and even take a refreshing dip in the ocean with

your significant other for a truly romantic adventure.

4. Zipline Canopy Tours:
   For the more adventurous couples, embark on a zipline canopy tour through the treetops of Jamaica's rainforests. Feel the adrenaline rush as you soar hand in hand, enjoying panoramic views and the thrill of this exhilarating experience.

5. Blue Hole Exploration:
   Discover the hidden gem of the Blue Hole, a secluded series of natural limestone pools surrounded by lush vegetation. Dive into the azure waters together, swim beneath cascading waterfalls, and relish the tranquility of this romantic oasis.

6. Private Waterfall Picnic:
   Arrange a private picnic at one of Jamaica's picturesque waterfalls. Enjoy a secluded spot with gourmet treats while being serenaded by the soothing sounds of nature, creating an intimate and unforgettable moment.

7. Candlelit Dinner at Rick's Café:
   Head to Rick's Café for a romantic candlelit dinner with a breathtaking view of the sunset. Indulge in delectable Jamaican cuisine while

savoring the company of your loved one against the backdrop of the Caribbean Sea.

These couple-friendly adventures in Jamaica are designed to enhance the bond between partners, providing a perfect blend of romance and excitement on this tropical paradise. Whether seeking serenity or adventure, Jamaica offers an idyllic setting for couples to create cherished memories together.

C. *Intimate Dining and Nightlife*

Discover the enchanting allure of Jamaica's intimate dining and vibrant nightlife, where the island's rich culture comes alive after the sun sets.

1. Romantic Dining Experiences:
   A. Seaside Retreats: Indulge in candlelit dinners at beachfront restaurants, savoring fresh seafood while gentle waves provide a romantic soundtrack.
   B. Hillside Hideaways: Explore charming mountaintop eateries offering panoramic views, creating an intimate ambiance for couples.

2. Local Flavors and Cuisine:
   A. Jamaican Fusion: Delight your taste buds with fusion cuisine, blending traditional Jamaican

flavors with international influences, creating a culinary symphony.

B. Street Food Adventures: Dive into the local scene with street food markets, where authentic flavors and lively atmospheres provide an unforgettable experience.

3. Live Music and Entertainment:
A. Reggae Vibes: Immerse yourself in the soulful rhythms of reggae at renowned music venues, where live performances capture the essence of Jamaican music culture.

B. Jazz and Blues Evenings: Enjoy sophisticated evenings at jazz and blues clubs, showcasing local and international talents against the backdrop of Jamaica's vibrant nightlife.

4. Chic Bars and Lounges:
A. Trendy Hotspots: Experience the modern side of Jamaica at chic bars and lounges, offering craft cocktails and trendy atmospheres for a stylish night out.

B. Rooftop Retreats: Elevate your evening at rooftop bars, providing panoramic views of the city lights and starlit skies, perfect for a romantic night with your significant other.

5. Cultural Events and Festivals:

A. Night Markets: Engage in the lively atmosphere of night markets, where you can explore local crafts, art, and music, immersing yourself in Jamaica's vibrant cultural scene.

B. Festive Celebrations: Plan your visit around local festivals and celebrations, where the streets come alive with music, dance, and a palpable sense of community.

Jamaica's intimate dining and nightlife scene offers a perfect blend of romance, culture, and entertainment, ensuring unforgettable experiences for couples seeking a memorable getaway.

Chapter V. Hidden Gems

A. *Off-the-Beaten-Path Attractions*

Venture beyond the typical tourist spots to discover the lesser-known, off-the-beaten-path attractions that unveil the authentic charm of Jamaica. In this part, we delve into secluded gems that promise a unique and enriching experience for the intrepid traveler.

1. Blue Hole in Ocho Rios:
   Embark on a journey to the Blue Hole, a mesmerizing series of natural limestone pools surrounded by lush greenery. This secluded oasis offers a refreshing escape and the chance to cliff jump into crystal-clear waters. A hidden paradise for nature lovers and thrill-seekers alike.

2. YS Falls in St. Elizabeth:
   Nestled in the lush countryside, YS Falls is a captivating seven-tiered waterfall. Away from the crowds, visitors can enjoy the serenity of the surrounding rainforest and take a dip in the cool, natural pools. A tranquil retreat for those seeking a peaceful communion with nature.

3. Mayfield Falls in Westmoreland:

Discover the enchanting Mayfield Falls, where a guided tour takes you through a riverbed adorned with terraced natural pools and mini waterfalls. This offbeat attraction allows you to connect with Jamaica's tropical beauty while enjoying a more secluded atmosphere.

4. Mavis Bank Coffee Factory Tour:
For a unique cultural experience, venture to the Blue Mountains and explore the Mavis Bank Coffee Factory. Engage in an informative tour to witness the coffee production process and savor some of the finest Jamaican coffee. A must-visit for coffee enthusiasts seeking an off-the-beaten-path adventure.

5. Alligator Pond in Manchester:
Escape the crowds and head to Alligator Pond, a tranquil fishing village with a distinct charm. Relax on the pristine beaches, savor fresh seafood at local eateries, and witness the daily life of the friendly community. A hidden coastal gem, perfect for those craving an authentic Jamaican experience.

Unearth the secrets of Jamaica by embracing these off-the-beaten-path attractions. Each destination promises a blend of natural beauty, cultural richness, and a sense of adventure that goes beyond the ordinary tourist trail. Take the road less traveled and create memories that linger long after your Jamaican journey.

B. Local Favorites and Cultural Gems

Discovering Jamaica's vibrant culture goes beyond the tourist hotspots, offering a rich tapestry of local favorites and hidden gems. Immerse yourself in the heartbeat of the island with these authentic experiences:

1. Trench Town - Birthplace of Reggae:
   Explore Trench Town, the iconic neighborhood in Kingston where reggae music was born. Visit the Bob Marley Museum to delve into the life and legacy of the reggae legend. Engage with local artists and musicians who continue to shape Jamaica's musical landscape.

2. Port Royal - Pirate's Haven:
   Uncover the history of Port Royal, once known as the "wickedest city on earth." Delight in the intriguing Pirate Museum, showcasing artifacts from the golden age of piracy. Stroll through historic streets and feel the echoes of swashbuckling tales in this charming coastal town.

3. Jamaican Maroons - Living History:

Connect with Jamaica's Maroon communities, descendants of escaped slaves who established independent societies. Discover their unique culture, marked by vibrant music, dance, and traditional ceremonies. Accompany locals on a trek through the lush Cockpit Country, gaining insight into their remarkable history.

4. Jamaican Jerk Trail:
Embark on a flavorful journey along the Jamaican Jerk Trail, where you can savor the island's signature spicy cuisine. From roadside jerk stands to renowned restaurants, experience the diverse interpretations of this beloved culinary tradition.

5. Street Art in Kingston:
Wander through the streets of Kingston to witness a burgeoning street art scene. Admire colorful murals and graffiti that reflect Jamaica's social and cultural narratives. Engage with local artists and learn about the inspirations behind their vibrant creations.

6. Martha Brae River Rafting:
Float serenely down the Martha Brae River on a bamboo raft steered by an expert raftsman. Enjoy the lush surroundings and discover the legends associated with this tranquil waterway. It's an

intimate and culturally immersive experience that reveals the natural beauty of Jamaica.

By embracing these local favorites and cultural gems, you'll forge a deeper connection with Jamaica, unlocking the essence of its people, history, and artistic expressions.

C. Serene Nature Escapes

Discovering Jamaica's vibrant culture goes beyond the tourist hotspots, offering a rich tapestry of local favorites and hidden gems. Immerse yourself in the heartbeat of the island with these authentic experiences:

1. Trench Town - Birthplace of Reggae:
   Explore Trench Town, the iconic neighborhood in Kingston where reggae music was born. Visit the Bob Marley Museum to delve into the life and legacy of the reggae legend. Engage with local artists and musicians who continue to shape Jamaica's musical landscape.

2. Port Royal - Pirate's Haven:
   Uncover the history of Port Royal, once known as the "wickedest city on earth." Delight in the intriguing Pirate Museum, showcasing artifacts from the golden age of piracy. Stroll through

historic streets and feel the echoes of swashbuckling tales in this charming coastal town.

3. Jamaican Maroons - Living History:
Connect with Jamaica's Maroon communities, descendants of escaped slaves who established independent societies. Discover their unique culture, marked by vibrant music, dance, and traditional ceremonies. Accompany locals on a trek through the lush Cockpit Country, gaining insight into their remarkable history.

4. Jamaican Jerk Trail:
Embark on a flavorful journey along the Jamaican Jerk Trail, where you can savor the island's signature spicy cuisine. From roadside jerk stands to renowned restaurants, experience the diverse interpretations of this beloved culinary tradition.

5. Street Art in Kingston:
Wander through the streets of Kingston to witness a burgeoning street art scene. Admire colorful murals and graffiti that reflect Jamaica's social and cultural narratives. Engage with local artists and learn about the inspirations behind their vibrant creations.

6. Martha Brae River Rafting:

Float serenely down the Martha Brae River on a bamboo raft steered by an expert raftsman. Enjoy the lush surroundings and discover the legends associated with this tranquil waterway. It's an intimate and culturally immersive experience that reveals the natural beauty of Jamaica.

By embracing these local favorites and cultural gems, you'll forge a deeper connection with Jamaica, unlocking the essence of its people, history, and artistic expressions.

Chapter VI. Must-Visit Locations

A. Iconic Landmarks

Jamaica boasts a wealth of iconic landmarks that weave together the island's rich history and breathtaking natural beauty. Explore these must-visit sites to fully immerse yourself in the essence of Jamaica:

1. Dunn's River Falls:
   Cascading over limestone terraces, Dunn's River Falls is a natural wonder that invites visitors to climb its tiers for a refreshing and exhilarating experience. The lush surrounding greenery and the Caribbean Sea backdrop make it a picture-perfect destination.

2. Bob Marley Museum:
   Pay homage to the legendary reggae icon, Bob Marley, by visiting his former residence, now transformed into a museum. Immerse yourself in the reggae culture, learn about Marley's life, and feel the rhythm that defines Jamaica.

3. Blue Mountains and John Crow Mountains National Park:
   A UNESCO World Heritage Site, these majestic mountains provide a stunning backdrop to

Jamaica's landscape. Home to the world-famous Blue Mountain coffee, the area offers hiking trails, lush flora, and panoramic views.

4. Rose Hall Great House:
Uncover the mystique of the Rose Hall Great House, a historic plantation with tales of ghostly legends. Explore the opulent rooms, learn about its haunting history, and enjoy panoramic views of the Caribbean Sea.

5. Port Royal:
Once dubbed the "wickedest city on Earth," Port Royal is a historic harbor town with a notorious past. Visit the archaeological site to discover remnants of this pirate haven, submerged buildings, and artifacts that tell tales of its golden age.

6. Devon House:
Immerse yourself in colonial architecture and Jamaican history at Devon House. This mansion, built in 1881, provides a glimpse into the island's past. Indulge in the delectable treats at the on-site bakery or explore the lush gardens.

7. Mystic Mountain:

For adventure seekers, Mystic Mountain offers a thrilling experience with zip lines, bobsled rides, and a sky explorer chairlift. Enjoy panoramic views of Ocho Rios and the surrounding rainforest from this eco-friendly attraction.

These iconic landmarks not only showcase Jamaica's diverse heritage but also offer visitors a chance to create lasting memories against the backdrop of the island's natural wonders and cultural richness.

B. Historical Sites

Jamaica boasts a rich tapestry of history, and exploring its historical sites offers a captivating journey into the island's past. Here are some key historical sites to discover:

1. Port Royal
   - Explore the sunken city of Port Royal, once known as the "Wickedest City on Earth." Visit the Archaeological Museum and learn about its pirate-infested history, including the infamous earthquake of 1692.

2. Rose Hall Great House
   - Uncover the mystery of the Rose Hall Great House, known for its haunting tales of Annie

Palmer, the White Witch. Take a guided tour through this 18th-century mansion and its lush surroundings.

3. Spanish Town
   - Delve into Jamaica's colonial history by visiting Spanish Town, the former capital. Discover the historic Cathedral of St. Jago de la Vega, the Old Courthouse, and other remnants of the island's Spanish and British colonial periods.

4. Devon House
   - Step back in time at Devon House, an exquisite Georgian mansion in Kingston. Built in 1881, it reflects Jamaica's plantation era and offers a glimpse into the lives of the island's elite.

5. Falmouth Historic District
   - Wander through Falmouth's well-preserved historic district, known for its Georgian architecture. Explore the town's historic churches, the Falmouth Court House, and gain insights into its role as a thriving port in the 18th century.

6. Seville Great House and Heritage Park
   - Immerse yourself in Jamaica's Taino-Arawak heritage at Seville Great House. The site provides a

fascinating look at the island's indigenous history and the Spanish colonization era.

7. Bob Marley Museum
   - While primarily a tribute to the reggae legend, the Bob Marley Museum in Kingston is also located at the singer's former residence, which holds historical significance. Explore Marley's life and the cultural impact of reggae music.

These historical sites weave together the diverse threads of Jamaica's past, offering a profound understanding of the island's cultural heritage. Whether you're drawn to tales of pirates, colonial architecture, or the roots of reggae music, Jamaica's historical sites promise a journey through time.

C. Scenic Spots

Immerse yourself in the breathtaking beauty of Jamaica's scenic spots, where nature unfolds in a vivid tapestry of colors and landscapes. From lush mountains to pristine beaches, here are some must-visit locations that promise to captivate every traveler:

1. Blue Mountains
   - Witness sunrise at Blue Mountain Peak, the island's highest point.

- Explore the aromatic coffee plantations nestled in the mountainous terrain.

2. Dunn's River Falls
   - Experience the sheer majesty of cascading water as you climb this iconic waterfall.
   - Discover hidden pools and refreshing lagoons along the way.

3. Seven Mile Beach
   - Relax on the powdery white sands of Negril's famous Seven Mile Beach.
   - Enjoy turquoise waters and vibrant sunsets that paint the sky in warm hues.

4. YS Falls
   - Immerse yourself in the tranquility of YS Falls, surrounded by lush rainforest.
   - Take a refreshing dip in natural pools fed by cascading waterfalls.

5. Reach Falls
   - Venture off the beaten path to Reach Falls, known for its emerald pools and enchanting bamboo groves.
   - Take a guided tour to uncover hidden caves and underwater passages.

6. Black River
   - Embark on a boat tour along the Black River, surrounded by mangroves and tropical birdlife.
   - Encounter crocodiles in their natural habitat during this unique eco-adventure.

7. Mystic Mountain
   - Soar above the treetops on a thrilling zipline adventure at Mystic Mountain.
   - Enjoy panoramic views of Ocho Rios and the Caribbean Sea from the Sky Explorer.

8. Fern Gully
   - Drive through the enchanting Fern Gully, a winding road shaded by a canopy of towering ferns.
   - Discover the diverse flora and fauna that thrive in this captivating rainforest corridor.

Whether you seek adventure, relaxation, or a blend of both, Jamaica's scenic wonders offer an unforgettable journey into the heart of the Caribbean's natural splendor.

Chapter VII. Itineraries

A. *One-Week Adventure*

Day 1: Arrival in Montego Bay
   - Morning: Arrive at Sangster International Airport
   - Afternoon: Relax at Doctor's Cave Beach
   - Evening: Explore the vibrant Hip Strip for dining and entertainment

Day 2: Montego Bay Adventures
   - Morning: Visit Rose Hall Great House
   - Afternoon: Zipline adventure at Mystic Mountain
   - Evening: Sunset dinner cruise from Montego Bay

Day 3: Ocho Rios Excursions
   - Morning: Dunn's River Falls and Park
   - Afternoon: Explore Dolphin Cove
   - Evening: Ocho Rios town for local cuisine

Day 4: Negril's Relaxing Vibes
   - Morning: Transfer to Negril
   - Afternoon: Enjoy Seven Mile Beach
   - Evening: Sunset at Rick's Cafe with cliff diving

Day 5: Cultural Day in Kingston

- Morning: Drive to Kingston
   - Afternoon: Visit Bob Marley Museum and Devon House
   - Evening: Explore nightlife in New Kingston

Day 6: Port Antonio Nature Escape
   - Morning: Drive to Port Antonio
   - Afternoon: Blue Lagoon and Frenchman's Cove
   - Evening: Enjoy local seafood in Port Antonio

Day 7: Beach Day and Departure
   - Morning: Relax on San San Beach
   - Afternoon: Last-minute shopping
   - Evening: Depart from Norman Manley International Airport

Note: This itinerary offers a mix of adventure, relaxation, cultural experiences, and diverse landscapes to provide a well-rounded exploration of Jamaica. Adjustments can be made based on personal preferences and interests.

B. Weekend Getaway Plans

Day 1: Exploring Kingston's Rich Heritage

Morning:
1. Start your day with a visit to the Bob Marley Museum to delve into Jamaica's reggae legacy.

2. Head to Devon House for a taste of Jamaican history and enjoy a traditional Jamaican breakfast.

Afternoon:
3. Explore the National Gallery of Jamaica to appreciate the island's vibrant art scene.
4. Have lunch at Gloria's Seafood, savoring delicious Jamaican seafood by the waterfront.

Evening:
5. Take a stroll through Emancipation Park for a relaxing atmosphere.
6. Enjoy dinner at the Terra Nova All-Suite Hotel for a blend of sophistication and Jamaican flavors.

Day 2: Ocho Rios Adventure

Morning:
1. Early departure to Ocho Rios, stopping at Scotchies for a hearty Jamaican jerk breakfast.
2. Visit Dunn's River Falls for a refreshing climb amid stunning natural surroundings.

Afternoon:
3. Have lunch at Bamboo Blu, a beachside restaurant with a relaxed atmosphere.
4. Explore Mystic Mountain for thrilling activities like zip-lining and bobsledding.

Evening:
5. Relax at Turtle River Park or stroll through Ocho Rios Craft Park.
6. Dine at Evita's Italian Restaurant, offering a romantic setting and delectable cuisine.

Day 3: Montego Bay Relaxation

Morning:
1. Travel to Montego Bay, stopping at Pelican Bar for a unique bar experience in the sea.
2. Breakfast at The HouseBoat Grill for a scenic start to your day.

Afternoon:
3. Spend the afternoon at Doctor's Cave Beach for sun and relaxation.
4. Enjoy lunch at Marguerite's Seafood by the waterfront.

Evening:
5. Explore the vibrant Hip Strip for shopping and local entertainment.
6. Conclude your weekend with a delightful dinner at Scotchies Montego Bay.

Note: Adjustments can be made based on personal preferences and travel constraints. Always check local guidelines and opening hours.

C. Customizable Itinerary Options

1. Adventure Seekers' Paradise (7 Days)

  - Day 1: Arrival in Montego Bay
    - Explore the Hip Strip
    - Relax at Doctor's Cave Beach

  - Day 2: Ocho Rios Excursion
    - Visit Dunn's River Falls
    - Experience Mystic Mountain

  - Day 3: Negril's Sunset Bliss
    - Head to Negril
    - Enjoy the sunset at Rick's Café

  - Day 4: Blue Mountains Trek
    - Journey to the Blue Mountains
    - Hike to the Blue Mountain Peak

  - Day 5: Port Antonio Bliss
    - Explore Frenchman's Cove
    - Discover Reach Falls

  - Day 6: Kingston Culture Day

- Visit Bob Marley Museum
- Explore Devon House

- Day 7: Departure from Kingston

2. Relaxation Retreat (5 Days)

    - Day 1: Arrival in Negril
        - Relax at Seven Mile Beach
        - Sunset Catamaran Cruise

    - Day 2: Day at Leisure
        - Spa Day or Water Activities

    - Day 3: Ocho Rios Serenity
        - Visit Konoko Falls
        - Explore Fern Gully

    - Day 4: Tranquil Port Antonio
        - Frenchman's Cove Relaxation
        - Blue Lagoon Boat Tour

    - Day 5: Departure from Montego Bay

3. Cultural Immersion (3 Days)

    - Day 1: Arrival in Kingston
        - Explore National Gallery of Jamaica

   - Enjoy local cuisine in Kingston

 - Day 2: Historic Tour
   - Visit Port Royal
   - Explore Spanish Town

 - Day 3: Departure from Kingston

Customize these itineraries based on your preferences, adding or adjusting activities to make the most of your Jamaican experience.

Chapter VIII. Culinary Delights

A. Jamaican Cuisine Overview

Indulge your taste buds in the vibrant and flavorful world of Jamaican cuisine, a delightful fusion of African, Spanish, British, Indian, and Chinese influences. From the aromatic jerk spices to the tropical sweetness of fresh fruits, Jamaican dishes reflect the island's rich cultural tapestry. Here's a glimpse into the culinary wonders awaiting you:

1. Jerk Delights:
  - Discover the world-famous Jamaican jerk seasoning, a spicy blend of Scotch bonnet peppers, allspice, thyme, and more.
  - Savor jerk chicken, pork, or fish grilled to perfection, offering a tantalizing combination of smokiness and heat.

2. Ackee and Saltfish:
  - Dive into Jamaica's national dish, Ackee and Saltfish, a unique blend of the creamy ackee fruit and salted cod, seasoned with onions, tomatoes, and spices.

3. Curry Infusions:

- Enjoy the aromatic allure of Jamaican curries, with goat, chicken, or seafood taking center stage in robust, flavorful stews.

4. Rice and Peas:
   - Delight in the staple side dish of rice and peas, where coconut milk, thyme, and scallion infuse the grains with a distinctive Caribbean flair.

5. Seafood Extravaganza:
   - Explore the bounties of the surrounding seas with fresh catches like escovitch fish, fried festival dumplings, and bammy, a flatbread made from cassava.

6. Patty Perfection:
   - Snack on Jamaican patties, flaky pastries filled with spiced meat, vegetables, or seafood, offering a portable burst of authentic island flavors.

7. Tropical Fruits:
   - Immerse yourself in the tropical abundance of fresh fruits like mangoes, papayas, pineapples, and coconuts, available in vibrant street markets and local stalls.

8. Rum-infused Delights:

- Toast to your Jamaican experience with locally produced rum, and don't miss out on desserts like rum cake, a decadent treat infused with the rich flavors of the Caribbean's signature spirit.

Jamaican cuisine is not just a meal; it's a sensory journey through the heart of the island's diverse history and culture. Whether you're a spice enthusiast, a seafood lover, or simply seeking culinary adventures, Jamaica's vibrant food scene promises an unforgettable gastronomic experience.

B. Best Local Eateries

When exploring Jamaica, indulging in the vibrant and flavorful local cuisine is a must. The island's culinary scene boasts a rich tapestry of tastes, blending influences from African, Indian, and European traditions. Here are some of the best local eateries to savor the authentic flavors of Jamaica:

1. Scotchies Jerk Center:
   Nestled in the heart of Montego Bay, Scotchies is a renowned jerk center that tantalizes taste buds with its smoky and perfectly spiced jerk chicken, pork, and fish. The casual outdoor setting enhances the laid-back Jamaican dining experience.

2. Pepper's Jerk Center:

Located in Ocho Rios, Pepper's Jerk Center is celebrated for its mouthwatering jerk dishes. The jerk-seasoned lobster is a standout, offering a delightful fusion of Jamaican spices with the island's abundant seafood.

3. Devon House I-Scream:

Indulge your sweet tooth at Devon House I-Scream in Kingston. This historic mansion serves up delectable homemade ice cream in a variety of tropical flavors. The lush surroundings of Devon House add to the charm of this delightful dessert haven.

4. Little Ochie Seafood Restaurant:

Positioned along the southern coast in Alligator Pond, Little Ochie is a seafood lover's paradise. This rustic seaside eatery offers an array of freshly caught fish, lobster, and shrimp, prepared in traditional Jamaican fashion.

5. Pelican Bar:

For a unique dining experience, venture to Pelican Bar, a rustic wooden structure perched on a sandbar in Parottee Bay. Accessible only by boat, this bar serves up fresh seafood and refreshing drinks amidst breathtaking ocean views.

6. Norma's at the Marina:
In the picturesque town of Port Antonio, Norma's at the Marina is a culinary gem. Helmed by renowned chef Norma Shirley, the restaurant combines Jamaican and international flavors, creating a sophisticated yet authentic dining experience.

7. Juici Patties:
For a quick and satisfying bite, don't miss Juici Patties. With multiple locations across the island, this chain is famous for its delicious patties filled with various savory fillings, making it a popular choice for locals and visitors alike.

Exploring these local eateries provides not only a gastronomic adventure but also a cultural immersion into the heart and soul of Jamaica's culinary traditions. Bon appétit!

C. Street Food Exploration

Embark on a culinary adventure through the vibrant streets of Jamaica, where the essence of the island's flavors comes to life in every bite. From bustling markets to roadside stalls, the street food scene is a tapestry of rich and diverse tastes that captivate the senses. Here's a glimpse into the delectable world of Jamaican street food:

1. Jerk Chicken Delight:
   Indulge in the iconic Jamaican jerk chicken, marinated with a blend of aromatic spices and slow-cooked to perfection. Served hot off the grill, the smoky and spicy flavors create a taste sensation that is uniquely Jamaican.

2. Patty Paradise:
   Sample the renowned Jamaican patties, flaky pastries filled with flavorful combinations of spiced meats, vegetables, or even seafood. These handheld delights are perfect for a quick snack while exploring the lively streets.

3. Festival Fun:
   Experience the joy of festivals – sweet fried dumplings that perfectly complement savory dishes. These golden-brown treats are often served alongside fried fish or jerk chicken, creating a delightful combination of textures and tastes.

4. Fresh Fruit Delights:
   Quench your thirst with refreshing coconut water or try exotic fruit slices seasoned with local spices. Embrace the tropical bounty as you stroll through markets where vibrant colors and tempting aromas beckon.

5. Bammy Bliss:

Discover bammy, a traditional Jamaican flatbread made from cassava. Often served with fish, bammy adds a unique texture and taste to your street food experience, offering a delightful departure from the ordinary.

6. Pepper Pot Soup:

Warm up your taste buds with a bowl of pepper pot soup, a hearty and spicy concoction that blends local vegetables, meats, and spices. It's a beloved comfort food that showcases Jamaica's diverse culinary influences.

7. Sugar Rush:

Treat your sweet tooth to Jamaican desserts like coconut drops, grater cake, or sweet potato pudding. These sweet delicacies reflect the island's sweet traditions, passed down through generations.

Navigating the lively street food scene in Jamaica not only provides a culinary adventure but also offers an authentic glimpse into the heart and soul of the island's culture. So, set aside any reservations, follow your nose, and let the vibrant world of Jamaican street food awaken your taste buds.

Chapter IX. Transportation and Getting Around

A. *Transportation Options*

Transportation in Jamaica offers a variety of options to explore the vibrant island.

1. Public Buses: Public buses are an affordable mode of transportation, connecting major towns and cities. While they might be a bit crowded, they provide an authentic Jamaican travel experience.

2. Route Taxis: Commonly referred to as "route taxis" or "shared taxis," these are an efficient way to travel between towns. They follow established routes and are recognizable by their red license plates. It's a shared ride, making it cost-effective.

3. Private Taxis: Private taxis are readily available and offer a more personalized travel experience. Negotiate fares in advance and ensure the taxi has a red license plate, indicating it's a registered and legal service.

4. Car Rentals: Renting a car provides flexibility, allowing you to explore Jamaica at your own pace. International and local car rental agencies operate

at airports and major tourist hubs. Be aware of local driving customs and road conditions.

5. JUTA Tours: The Jamaica Union of Travellers Association (JUTA) offers organized tours and transportation services. Ideal for those who prefer guided experiences, JUTA ensures reliable transportation for sightseeing and excursions.

6. Motorbike Rentals: For the adventurous traveler, renting a motorbike or scooter is an exhilarating way to explore the island. It provides the freedom to navigate through scenic routes independently.

7. Domestic Flights: While Jamaica is a relatively small island, domestic flights are available for those who want to save time on longer journeys. Small airports connect major cities and tourist destinations.

8. Bicycles: Some areas, especially along the coast, offer bicycle rentals. It's an eco-friendly and leisurely way to explore local neighborhoods and scenic routes.

9. Boat and Ferry Services: Given its coastal geography, water taxis and ferry services are

available for island-hopping or reaching places like Port Royal and the Pelican Bar.

Remember to plan transportation based on your preferences and the locations you intend to visit. Whether it's the bustling streets of Kingston or the laid-back beaches of Negril, Jamaica's diverse transportation options cater to every traveler's needs.

B. *Tips for Navigating Jamaica*

Navigating Jamaica: Practical Tips for Smooth Travel

1. Transportation Options:
   a. Explore public transportation like route taxis and buses for an authentic experience.
   b. Consider renting a car for more flexibility, especially if you plan to explore off-the-beaten-path destinations.

2. Navigating Cities:
   a. Embrace local landmarks and street signs for guidance in urban areas.
   b. Utilize GPS apps on your smartphone to navigate with ease.

3. Understanding Local Culture:

   a. Embrace the laid-back atmosphere; things might move at a slower pace than you're accustomed to.

   b. Engage with locals for directions or recommendations; Jamaicans are known for their friendliness.

4. Currency and Transactions:

   a. Have some Jamaican dollars for small purchases; larger establishments usually accept credit cards.

   b. Inform your bank about your travel dates to avoid any issues with card transactions.

5. Safety Precautions:

   a. Stay in well-traveled areas, especially at night.

   b. Keep belongings secure, and be mindful of your surroundings in crowded places.

6. Communication Essentials:

   a. Learn basic Jamaican Patois phrases for a more immersive experience.

   b. Purchase a local SIM card for your phone to stay connected without incurring high roaming charges.

7. Weather Considerations:

   a. Check weather forecasts before planning outdoor activities, as Jamaica can experience sudden rain showers.
   b. Pack accordingly, considering the tropical climate.

8. Respect Local Customs:
   a. Dress modestly when visiting religious or rural areas.
   b. Respect local customs and traditions, including greetings and etiquette.

9. Health and Safety:
   a. Stay hydrated in the tropical climate; drink bottled or purified water.
   b. Use sunscreen and insect repellent to protect yourself from the sun and mosquitoes.

10. Explore Off-the-Beaten-Path:
   a. Venture beyond popular tourist spots for a more authentic experience.
   b. Seek advice from locals or fellow travelers for hidden gems.

Remember, navigating Jamaica is not just about reaching your destination but savoring the journey filled with vibrant culture and breathtaking landscapes.

Chapter X. Cultural Insights

A. *Jamaican Traditions*

Jamaica's rich cultural tapestry is woven with vibrant traditions that reflect the island's history and diversity. Immerse yourself in the following Jamaican traditions for an authentic experience:

1. Reggae Rhythms:
   Embrace the soul-stirring beats of reggae music, a genre born on the streets of Kingston. Attend live performances, visit music festivals, and feel the rhythm that permeates the Jamaican air.

2. Rastafarian Influence:
   Explore the roots of Rastafari, a spiritual and cultural movement indigenous to Jamaica. Engage with locals to gain insights into their beliefs, marked by a reverence for nature, communal living, and the iconic dreadlocks.

3. Jamaican Patois:
   Immerse yourself in the unique linguistic flair of Jamaican Patois, a creole language that blends English with African, Spanish, and indigenous influences. Engaging with locals in Patois adds a delightful layer to your cultural experience.

4. Jerk Cuisine:

Indulge in the culinary tradition of jerk, a distinctive method of seasoning and grilling meats. Savor the flavorful dishes at local jerk stands, and perhaps, even attend a jerk festival to celebrate this mouthwatering tradition.

5. Maroon Heritage:

Discover the Maroons, descendants of runaway slaves who established free communities in Jamaica's rugged mountains. Engage in Maroon traditions through guided tours, storytelling, and experiencing their unique style of drumming and dancing.

6. Nyabinghi Drumming:

Immerse yourself in the powerful beats of Nyabinghi drumming, an essential element of Rastafarian celebrations. Experience drumming sessions at local gatherings, where rhythmic vibrations connect participants with spiritual roots.

7. Nine-Night Celebrations:

Attend a Nine-Night ceremony, a Jamaican tradition where family and friends gather to celebrate the life of a departed loved one. This cultural practice involves music, dance, and storytelling, creating a vibrant tribute to the deceased.

8. Junkanoo Parades:
   Experience the lively and colorful Junkanoo parades, which occur during festivals and celebrations. These processions feature elaborate costumes, lively music, and dance, showcasing the exuberance of Jamaican culture.

Participating in these traditions allows travelers to connect with Jamaica's soul, fostering a deeper appreciation for the island's cultural heritage.

B. Festivals and Events

Jamaica's vibrant culture comes alive through its diverse and lively festivals and events. Immerse yourself in the rhythmic beats and colorful celebrations that showcase the island's rich heritage.

1. Reggae Sumfest:
   - A world-renowned reggae music festival held annually in Montego Bay.
   - Showcasing local and international artists, it's a must-attend for music enthusiasts.

2. Jamaica Carnival:

- A lively and colorful celebration with vibrant parades and elaborate costumes.
- Features soca and dancehall music, providing an unforgettable experience for attendees.

3. Jamaica Independence Day:
   - Celebrated on August 6th, commemorating the country's independence from British rule.
   - Festivities include parades, cultural events, and a strong sense of national pride.

4. Maroon Festival:
   - Honoring the Maroons, descendants of escaped slaves who established independent communities.
   - Features traditional drumming, dancing, and storytelling, providing insight into Jamaica's history.

5. Jamaica Film Festival:
   - Showcasing the island's emerging talent in the film industry.
   - Attendees can enjoy screenings, workshops, and engage with filmmakers.

6. Jamaica Jazz and Blues Festival:
   - A fusion of jazz, blues, and reggae, attracting international and local artists.

- Offers a diverse musical experience in a captivating outdoor setting.

7. Accompong Maroon Festival:
  - Celebrated in Accompong, the oldest Maroon settlement in Jamaica.
  - Highlights include traditional Maroon ceremonies, cultural displays, and a sense of unity.

8. Bob Marley Birthday Celebration:
  - Honoring the legendary reggae icon's birthday on February 6th.
  - Features concerts, parties, and events paying homage to Bob Marley's enduring influence.

9. Portland Jerk Festival:
  - Showcasing Jamaica's famous jerk cuisine in the picturesque parish of Portland.
  - A flavorful experience with live music, culinary competitions, and a vibrant atmosphere.

10. Ocho Rios Jazz Festival:
  - Bringing smooth jazz melodies to the scenic coastal town of Ocho Rios.
  - Offers a laid-back atmosphere and a perfect blend of music and tropical surroundings.

When planning your visit, check the festival calendar to align your trip with these dynamic events, ensuring an immersive and culturally enriching experience in Jamaica.

C. Interacting with Locals

Interacting with Locals in Jamaica:

1. Embrace the Laid-Back Vibe:
   Jamaicans are known for their easygoing and friendly nature. Take a cue from the locals and embrace the laid-back atmosphere. Engage in casual conversations, and don't be afraid to share a smile or a friendly greeting.

2. Respect the Culture:
   Show respect for Jamaican customs and traditions. Familiarize yourself with common greetings like "respect" and "bless up." Understanding and acknowledging the local culture will enhance your connections with the community.

3. Strike Up Conversations:
   Jamaicans are generally open and welcoming. Strike up conversations with locals at markets, cafes, or community events. Ask about their favorite spots or recommendations – locals often provide valuable insights that may lead you to hidden gems.

4. Participate in Local Activities:

   Joining in on local activities and events can be a fantastic way to connect with residents. Whether it's a community celebration, a reggae concert, or a street festival, participating in these events will offer you a glimpse into the lively Jamaican spirit.

5. Support Local Businesses:

   Choose locally-owned establishments for dining, shopping, and entertainment. Engaging with local businesses not only supports the community but also provides opportunities for authentic interactions with the people who call Jamaica home.

6. Learn Some Patois Phrases:

   While English is the official language, Jamaican Patois is widely spoken and cherished. Learning a few basic Patois phrases can be a fun way to break the ice and connect with locals on a more personal level.

7. Be Open to Invitations:

   Jamaicans are known for their hospitality. If you receive an invitation to join a local gathering or event, consider accepting. It's a chance to experience Jamaican hospitality firsthand and create lasting memories.

8. Respect Personal Space:
While Jamaicans are warm and welcoming, it's essential to be mindful of personal space. Respect cultural boundaries, and approach interactions with genuine curiosity and friendliness.

By embracing the rich tapestry of Jamaican culture and engaging with its people, you'll not only enhance your travel experience but also leave with lasting memories and perhaps some newfound friendships.

Chapter XI. Practical Information

A. *Currency and Money Matters*

Jamaica's official currency is the Jamaican Dollar (JMD). When traveling to Jamaica, it's essential to be aware of the local currency and the country's financial landscape. Here are some key considerations for managing currency and money matters during your stay:

1. Currency Exchange:
   - Exchange rates can fluctuate, so it's advisable to check for the latest rates before exchanging money.
   - Currency exchange services are widely available at airports, banks, and authorized exchange bureaus.

2. Credit Cards and ATMs:
   - Major credit cards, such as Visa and MasterCard, are widely accepted in tourist areas, hotels, and restaurants.
   - ATMs are also prevalent in urban areas and tourist spots, providing a convenient way to withdraw Jamaican Dollars. Be cautious about transaction fees, and inform your bank about your travel plans to avoid card issues.

3. Cash Usage:

- While cards are accepted in many places, having some Jamaican Dollars in cash is advisable for small purchases, local markets, and places that may not accept cards.

4. Tipping Etiquette:
 - Tipping is customary in Jamaica. It is customary to tip around 10-15% in restaurants, and it's common to tip service providers such as tour guides and drivers.

5. Budgeting Tips:
 - Establish a daily budget to manage your expenses effectively.
 - Prices in tourist areas may be higher than in local markets, so exploring different areas can offer a range of options.

6. Bargaining:
 - Bargaining is a common practice in local markets, but it may not be as prevalent in established stores. Politeness is key during negotiations.

7. Currency Restrictions:
 - There are no restrictions on the amount of foreign currency you can bring into Jamaica.

However, amounts exceeding USD 10,000 or its equivalent must be declared.

By familiarizing yourself with these currency and money matters, you'll be better equipped to navigate Jamaica's financial landscape and make the most of your travel experience.

B. Health and Safety

Jamaica is a vibrant destination, and ensuring your well-being during your stay is crucial. Here are key aspects to consider for a safe and healthy experience:

1. Medical Facilities:
   - Familiarize yourself with local hospitals and medical clinics.
   - Check if your accommodation has access to medical services or a first aid kit.

2. Travel Insurance:
   - Obtain comprehensive travel insurance that covers medical emergencies.
   - Keep a copy of your insurance policy and emergency contact information readily available.

3. Vaccinations and Health Precautions:

- Consult your healthcare provider for recommended vaccinations before traveling.
- Use insect repellent to guard against mosquito-borne illnesses like dengue and Zika.

4. Water Safety:
- Consume bottled or purified water to avoid waterborne illnesses.
- Be cautious when swimming, adhere to local advisories, and avoid strong currents.

5. Sun Protection:
- Jamaica's tropical climate calls for sun protection measures.
- Pack sunscreen, hats, and light clothing to shield yourself from the sun.

6. Food Safety:
- Enjoy the local cuisine, but choose reputable eateries to minimize food-related risks.
- Wash hands regularly and practice good hygiene to prevent foodborne illnesses.

7. Crime Awareness:
- Exercise caution in urban areas and tourist spots.
- Keep valuables secure and be mindful of your surroundings, especially in crowded places.

8. Local Laws and Customs:
   - Familiarize yourself with Jamaican laws and respect local customs.
   - Be aware of restrictions on certain activities or substances.

9. Emergency Numbers:
   - Save important contact numbers, including local emergency services and your country's embassy or consulate.

10. Environmental Awareness:
    - Respect the natural surroundings and wildlife.
    - Follow any guidelines provided at nature reserves or protected areas.

Remember, staying informed and being vigilant contributes significantly to a safe and enjoyable visit to Jamaica. Embrace the local culture and scenery while prioritizing your health and well-being.

C. Communication Essentials

When visiting Jamaica, effective communication is key to enriching your travel experience. Here are some essentials to keep in mind:

1. Language:
   - The official language is English, making communication easy for most travelers.
   - Jamaican Patois, a local creole, is also widely spoken. Familiarizing yourself with common phrases can enhance interactions and local connections.

2. Greetings and Customs:
   - A warm and friendly demeanor is appreciated. Greet people with a smile and a simple "Good morning," "Good afternoon," or "Good evening."
   - Handshakes are common, and it's polite to maintain eye contact during conversations.

3. Respectful Communication:
   - Jamaicans value respect and courtesy. Using "please" and "thank you" goes a long way in interactions.
   - Engage in conversations with genuine interest, and be open to the laid-back and friendly Jamaican communication style.

4. Local Slang and Expressions:
   - Embrace the local flavor by incorporating some Jamaican slang into your conversations. For example, "irie" means everything is good or cool.

5. Understanding Dialects:
   - Different regions in Jamaica may have distinct dialects or variations in pronunciation. Embrace the diversity and ask locals for guidance if needed.

6. Communication in Rural Areas:
   - In rural areas, English may not be as prevalent. Basic phrases in Patois can be especially useful in these settings.

7. Technology and Connectivity:
   - Ensure your mobile phone is compatible with Jamaican networks. Local SIM cards are readily available for purchase if needed.
   - Free Wi-Fi is commonly available in hotels and restaurants, but connectivity may vary in more remote areas.

8. Emergency Phrases:
   - Familiarize yourself with emergency phrases and contact numbers. Knowing how to seek help in case of unforeseen circumstances is crucial.

Remember, communication is not just about words but also about cultural understanding and openness. Engaging with locals in a respectful and friendly manner will undoubtedly enhance your Jamaican experience.

D. Emergency Contacts

Emergency Contacts in Jamaica:

1. Emergency Services:
   - Police: 119
   - Ambulance/Fire Department: 110
   - Jamaica Tourist Board (24/7 Hotline): +1 876-936-0715

2. Medical Assistance:
   - Public Hospitals: Contact the nearest one in case of medical emergencies.
   - Examples: Kingston Public Hospital, Cornwall Regional Hospital.
   - Private Medical Facilities: Check with your accommodation for recommended options.

3. Embassies and Consulates:
   - United States Embassy (Kingston): +1 876-702-6000
   - Canadian High Commission (Kingston): +1 876-926-1500
   - United Kingdom High Commission (Kingston): +1 876-936-0700

4. Roadside Assistance:
   - Island Traffic Authority (Accidents/Issues): +1 876-754-9263

- Automobile Association of Jamaica (24-Hour Emergency Service): +1 876-929-5869

5. Tourist Helpline:
   - Jamaica Tourist Board Emergency Line: +1 876-936-0715
   - Tourist Police (Available in Tourist Areas): Dial 311 or contact the nearest police station.

6. Natural Disaster and Weather Information:
   - Meteorological Service of Jamaica: +1 876-929-3694
   - Office of Disaster Preparedness and Emergency Management (ODPEM): +1 876-906-9674

7. Consular Services for Other Countries:
   - Check with your respective embassy or consulate for additional emergency contacts.

It's essential to have these contacts readily available during your stay in Jamaica to ensure a safe and swift response in case of any emergencies. Always exercise caution, stay informed, and reach out for assistance when needed.

Chapter XII. Conclusion

A. Share your experience

Celestial Rhythms: The Legend of Jamaica's Harmony Stones

In the heart of Jamaica, where the lush greenery meets the azure waters, there lies a mystical tale of the "Harmony Stones." Legend has it that centuries ago, when the island was newly formed, the spirits of the land and sea came together to create these enchanted stones to safeguard the unity and serenity of Jamaica.

It is said that each stone represents a different aspect of the island's spirit – the lively rhythm of reggae, the vibrant hues of the tropical flora, the warmth of the golden sun, and the soothing whispers of the Caribbean Sea. The Harmony Stones, scattered across hidden corners of Jamaica, emit a magical energy that resonates with the very essence of the island.

Travelers who embark on a quest to discover these stones are said to be bestowed with a special connection to Jamaica's soul. As the sun sets over the cliffs of Negril, seekers often gather around the Unity Stone, where the energies of the island converge. It is here that locals and visitors alike share stories, laughter, and the rhythmic beats of drums, reinforcing the harmony that binds them together.

So, as you explore the wonders of Jamaica, keep an eye out for these mystical Harmony Stones. Engage with the island's spirit, dance to the reggae tunes, and let the enchanting tale of unity guide your journey through this Caribbean paradise. For in the heart of Jamaica, the Harmony Stones whisper stories of joy, love, and the eternal connection between the land and those who tread upon it.

Printed in Dunstable, United Kingdom